I0814620

Jenna Ortega

Scream Queen & Star of *Wednesday*

by Grace Hansen

Abdo Kids Jumbo is an Imprint of Abdo Kids
abdobooks.com

abdobooks.com

Published by Abdo Kids, a division of ABDO, P.O. Box 398166, Minneapolis, Minnesota 55439.

Abdo Kids Jumbo™ is a trademark and logo of Abdo Kids.

Printed in China

052024

092024

Photo Credits: Alamy, AP Images, Everette Collection, Getty Images, Shutterstock

Production Contributors: Teddy Borth, Jennie Forsberg, Grace Hansen
Design Contributors: Candice Keimig, Pakou Moua

Library of Congress Control Number: 2023948671

Publisher's Cataloging-in-Publication Data

Names: Hansen, Grace, author.

Title: Jenna Ortega: scream queen & star of Wednesday / by Grace Hansen

Other title: scream queen & star of Wednesday

Description: Minneapolis, Minnesota : Abdo Kids, 2025 | Series: Leading biographies | Includes online resources and index.

Identifiers: ISBN 9798384900757 (lib. bdg.) | ISBN 9798384901457 (ebook) | ISBN 9798384901808 (Read-to-me eBook)

Subjects: LCSH: Ortega, Jenna--Juvenile literature. | Motion picture actors and actresses--Biography—Juvenile literature. | Actresses--Biography--Juvenile literature. | Addams, Wednesday (Fictitious character)--Juvenile literature.

Classification: DDC 791.43092--dc23

Table of Contents

Jenna's Beginnings

Jenna Marie Ortega was born on September 27, 2002. She grew up in Palm Desert, California, with her parents and five siblings.

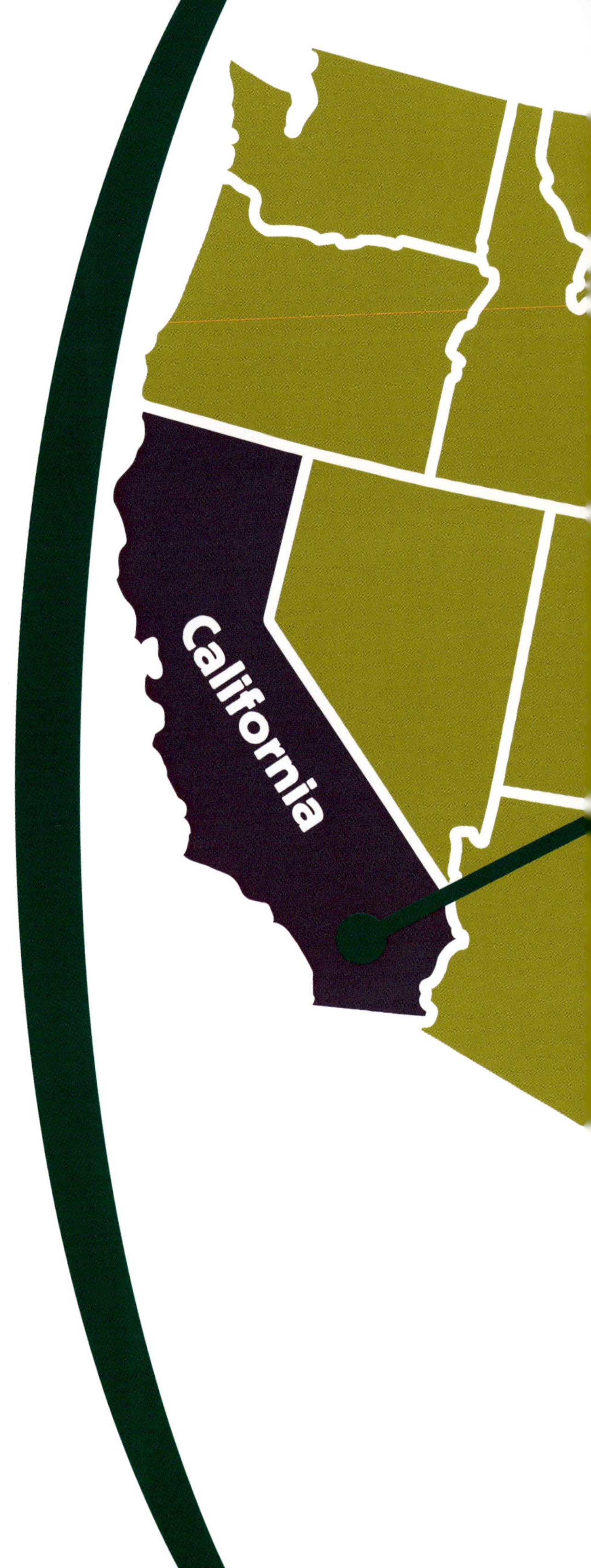

N
W
E
S
Palm Desert

From a young age, Jenna knew she wanted to act. When Jenna was 9, her mother filmed Jenna acting. She posted the video online. Soon, Jenna was signed to an **agency**!

Jenna and her mom

Landing Roles

Jenna left school in the 8th grade to focus on acting. She landed several roles in TV series and films.

Richie Rich TV series

In 2016, Jenna starred in her first TV series. Jenna played the lead role, inventor Harley Diaz, in Disney's *Stuck in the Middle* for three seasons.

MARSHPORT
TERRIERS

In 2018, Jenna was **cast** in *You*, a Netflix **thriller** series. She played Ellie Alves in the show's second season. Jenna enjoyed the creative freedom of the role.

LOVE
AH

In 2022, Jenna played characters in three **horror** films. People began to call her "the new '**it girl**' of horror."

MTV
Movie
&TV

Working as Wednesday

In May of 2021, Jenna was **cast** in the TV series *Wednesday*. Jenna took on the role of Wednesday Addams, a **psychic** teenager.

In January 2023, *Wednesday* was renewed for a second season. Jenna took on new roles overseeing writing and costumes for the show.

What's Next?

Jenna has found her place playing spookier roles. Fans are excited to watch as she continues to grow as an actress.

FOX
EMMYS

Career Highlights

2012 Jenna lands her first television role on the show *Rob*.

2013 Jenna acts in her first **blockbuster** movie, *Iron Man 3*.

January 2023 Jenna wins the Breakthrough Artist Award by the Austin Film Critics Association for her roles in four films.

March 2023 Jenna wins Favorite Female TV Star for her role as Wednesday at the Nickelodeon Kids' Choice Awards.

March 2023 Ortega hosts an episode of *Saturday Night Live*.

May 2023 Jenna wins Best Performance in a Show at the MTV Movie & TV Awards (*Wednesday*).

July 2023 Jenna is nominated for a Primetime Emmy Award for Outstanding Lead Actress in a Comedy Series (*Wednesday*).

2024 Jenna is set to star in and **executive produce** the romantic film *Winter Spring Summer or Fall*.

Glossary

agency – a company that does business in support of other people.

blockbuster – a film with an extremely high production and marketing budget.

cast – to be chosen for a part in a play or film.

executive produce – heading the production of a film or television show and finding and securing money and talent for the project.

horror – a genre of fiction that is meant to scare, startle, and shock audiences.

it girl – a famous young woman who is very popular.

psychic – a person sensitive to the nonphysical, spiritual, or supernatural.

thriller – a genre of fiction that is meant to induce strong feelings of excitement, anxiety, tension, and suspense in audiences.

Index